Also by Kenneth Koch

Poems

Ko, or A Season on Earth

Permanently

Thank You and Other Poems

Bertha and Other Plays

When the Sun Tries to Go On

The Pleasures of Peace

Wishes, Lies, and Dreams:
Teaching Children to Write Poetry

A Change of Hearts:
Plays, Films, and Other Dramatic Works

Rose, Where Did You Get That Red?
Teaching Great Poetry to Children

THE ART OF LOVE

THE ART OF LOVE

POEMS

by

KENNETH KOCH

VINTAGE BOOKS

A Division of Random House

New York

VINTAGE BOOKS, June 1975

All rights reserved under International and Pan-American Copyright
Conventions. Published in the United States by Random House, Inc.,
New York, and simultaneously in Canada by Random House of Canada
Limited, Toronto. Originally published by Random House, Inc., in
1975.
Parts I and II of "The Art of Love," "The Art of Poetry" and "On Beauty"
first appeared in *Poetry Magazine*; "The Circus," "Alive for
an Instant" and "Some General Instructions" first appeared in *The New York
Review of Books*.

Library of Congress Cataloging in Publication Data
Koch, Kenneth
The art of love: poems.

I. Title.
PS3521.O27A9 1975b   811'.5'4   74-30355
ISBN 0-394-71508-X

Manufactured in the United States of America

To Julie Whitaker

CONTENTS

THE ART OF LOVE

THE CIRCUS

I remember when I wrote The Circus
I was living in Paris, or rather we were living in Paris
Janice, Frank was alive, the Whitney Museum
Was still on 8th Street, or was it still something else?
Fernand Léger lived in our building
Well it wasn't really our building it was the building we
    lived in
Next to a Grand Guignol troupe who made a lot of
    noise
So that one day I yelled through a hole in the wall
Of our apartment I don't know why there was a hole
    there
Shut up! And the voice came back to me saying
    something
I don't know what. Once I saw Léger walk out of the
    building

I think. Stanley Kunitz came to dinner. I wrote The
    Circus
In two tries, the first getting most of the first stanza;
That fall I also wrote an opera libretto called Louisa or
    Matilda.
Jean-Claude came to dinner. He said (about "cocktail
    sauce")
It should be good on something but not on these
    (oysters).
By that time I think I had already written The Circus.
Part of the inspiration came while walking to the post
    office one night
And I wrote a big segment of The Circus
When I came back, having been annoyed to have to go
I forget what I went there about
You were back in the apartment what a dump actually
    we liked it
I think with your hair and your writing and the pans
Moving strummingly about the kitchen and I wrote
    The Circus
It was a summer night no it was an autumn one summer
    when
I remember it but actually no autumn that black dusk
    toward the post office
And I wrote many other poems then but The Circus
    was the best
Maybe not by far the best Geography was also wonder-
    ful
And the Airplane Betty poems (inspired by you) but
    The Circus was the best.

4

Sometimes I feel I actually am the person
Who did this, who wrote that, including that poem The
    Circus
But sometimes on the other hand I don't.
There are so many factors engaging our attention!
At every moment the happiness of others, the health of
    those we know and our own!
And the millions upon millions of people we don't
    know and their well-being to think about
So it seems strange I found time to write The Circus
And even spent two evenings on it, and that I have also
    the time
To remember that I did it, and remember you and me
    then, and write this poem about it
At the beginning of The Circus
The Circus girls are rushing through the night
In the circus wagons and tulips and other flowers will be
    picked
A long time from now this poem wants to get off on its
    own
Someplace like a painting not held to a depiction of
    composing The Circus.

Noel Lee was in Paris then but usually out of it
In Germany or Denmark giving a concert
As part of an endless activity
Which was either his career or his happiness or a
    combination of both
Or neither I remember his dark eyes looking he was
    nervous

5

With me perhaps because of our days at Harvard.

It is understandable enough to be nervous with any-
    body!

How softly and easily one feels when alone
Love of one's friends when one is commanding the time
    and space syndrome
If that's the right word which I doubt but together how
    come one is so nervous?
One is not always but what was I then and what am I
    now attempting to create
If create is the right word
Out of this combination of experience and aloneness
And who are you telling me it is or is not a poem (not
    you)? Go back with me though
To those nights I was writing The Circus.
Do you like that poem? have you read it? It is in my
    book Thank You
Which Grove just reprinted. I wonder how long I am
    going to live
And what the rest will be like I mean the rest of my life.

John Cage said to me the other night How old are you?
    and I told him forty-six
(Since then I've become forty-seven) he said
Oh that's a great age I remember.
John Cage once told me he didn't charge much for his
    mushroom identification course (at the New
    School)

Because he didn't want to make a profit from nature

He was ahead of his time I was behind my time we were
    both in time
Brilliant go to the head of the class and "time is a river"
It doesn't seem like a river to me it seems like an
    unformed plan
Days go by and still nothing is decided about
What to do until you know it never will be and then
    you say "time"
But you really don't care much about it any more
Time means something when you have the major part
    of yours ahead of you
As I did in Aix-en-Provence that was three years before I
    wrote The Circus
That year I wrote Bricks and The Great Atlantic
    Rainway
I felt time surround me like a blanket endless and soft
I could go to sleep endlessly and wake up and still be in
    it
But I treasured secretly the part of me that was
    individually changing
Like Noel Lee I was interested in my career
And still am but now it is like a town I don't want to
    leave
Not a tower I am climbing opposed by ferocious
    enemies

I never mentioned my friends in my poems at the time I
    wrote The Circus

Although they meant almost more than anything to me
Of this now for some time I've felt an attenuation
So I'm mentioning them maybe this will bring them
    back to me
Not them perhaps but what I felt about them
John Ashbery Jane Freilicher Larry Rivers Frank
    O'Hara
Their names alone bring tears to my eyes
As seeing Polly did last night

It is beautiful at any time but the paradox is leaving it
In order to feel it when you've come back the sun has
    declined
And the people are merrier or else they've gone home
    altogether
And you are left alone well you put up with that your
    sureness is like the sun
While you have it but when you don't its lack's a black
    and icy night. I came home

And wrote The Circus that night, Janice. I didn't come
    and speak to you
And put my arm around you and ask you if you'd like to
    take a walk
Or go to the Cirque Medrano though that's what I
    wrote poems about
And am writing about that now, and now I'm alone

And this is not as good a poem as The Circus
And I wonder if any good will come of either of them
    all the same.

THE MAGIC OF NUMBERS

The Magic of Numbers—1

How strange it was to hear the furniture being moved
    around in the apartment upstairs!
I was twenty-six, and you were twenty-two.

The Magic of Numbers—2

You asked me if I wanted to run, but I said no and
    walked on.
I was nineteen and you were seven.

The Magic of Numbers—3

Yes, but does X really like us?
We were both twenty-seven.

9

The Magic of Numbers—4

You look like Jerry Lewis (1950).

The Magic of Numbers—5

Grandfather and grandmother want you to go over to
    their house for dinner.
They were sixty-nine, and I was two and a half.

The Magic of Numbers—6

One day when I was twenty-nine years old I met you
    and nothing happened.

The Magic of Numbers—7

No, of course it wasn't I who came to the library!
Brown eyes, flushed cheeks, brown hair. I was twenty-
    nine, and you were sixteen.

The Magic of Numbers—8

After we made love one night in Rockport I went
    outside and kissed the road
I felt so carried away. I was twenty-three, and you were
    nineteen.

The Magic of Numbers—9

I was twenty-nine, and so were you. We had a very
    passionate time.
Everything I read turned into a story about you and me,
    and everything I did was turned into a poem.

ALIVE FOR AN INSTANT

I have a bird in my head and a pig in my stomach
And a flower in my genitals and a tiger in my genitals
And a lion in my genitals and I am after you but I have
    a song in my heart
And my song is a dove
I have a man in my hands I have a woman in my shoes
I have a landmark decision in my reason
I have a death rattle in my nose I have summer in my
    brain water
I have dreams in my toes
This is the matter with me and the hammer of my
    mother and father
Who created me with everything
But I lack calm I lack rose
Though I do not lack extreme delicacy of rose petal
Who is it that I wish to astonish?

In the birdcall I found a reminder of you
But it was thin and brittle and gone in an instant
Has nature set out to be a great entertainer?
Obviously not A great reproducer? A great Nothing?
Well I will leave that up to you
I have a knocking woodpecker in my heart and I think I
     have three souls
One for love one for poetry and one for acting out my
     insane self
Not insane but boring but perpendicular but untrue but
     true
The three rarely sing together take my hand it's active
The active ingredient in it is a touch
I am Lord Byron I am Percy Shelley I am Ariosto
I eat the bacon I went down the slide I have a
     thunderstorm in my inside I will never hate you
But how can this maelstrom be appealing? do you like
     menageries? my god
Most people want a man! So here I am
I have a pheasant in my reminders I have a goshawk in
     my clouds
Whatever is it which has led all these animals to you?
A resurrection? or maybe an insurrection? an inspira-
     tion?
I have a baby in my landscape and I have a wild rat in
     my secrets from you.

SOME GENERAL INSTRUCTIONS

Do not bake bread in an oven that is not made of stone
Or you risk having imperfect bread. Byron wrote,
"The greatest pleasure in life is drinking hock
And soda water the morning after, when one has
A hangover," or words to that effect. It is a
Pleasure, for me, of the past. I do not drink so much
Any more. And when I do, I am not in sufficiently good
Shape to enjoy the hock and seltzer in the morning.
I am envious of this pleasure as I think of it. Do not
You be envious. In fact I cannot tell envy
From wish and desire and sharing imperfectly
What others have got and not got. But *envy* is a good
    word
To use, as *hate* is, and *lust*, because they make their
    point
In the worst and most direct way, so that as a

13

Result one is able to deal with them and go on one's
    way.
I read *Don Juan* twenty years ago, and six years later
I wrote a poem in emulation of it. I began
Searching for another stanza but gave in
To the ottava rima after a while, after I'd tried
Some practice stanzas in it; it worked so well
It was too late to stop, it seemed to me. Do not
Be in too much of a hurry to emulate what
You admire. Sometimes it may take a number of years
Before you are ready, but there it is, building
Inside you, a constructing egg. Low-slung
Buildings are sometimes dangerous to walk in and
Out of. A building should be at least one foot and a half
Above one's height, so that if one leaps
In surprise or joy or fear, one's head will not be injured.
Very high ceilings such as those in Gothic
Churches are excellent for giving a spiritual feeling.
Low roofs make one feel like a mole in general. But
Smallish rooms can be cozy. Many tiny people
In a little room make an amusing sight. Large
Persons, both male and female, are best seen out of
    doors.
Ships sided against a canal's side may be touched and
Patted, but sleeping animals should not be, for
They may bite, in anger and surprise. Of all animals
The duck is seventeenth lowliest, the eagle not as high
On the list as one would imagine, rating
Only ninety-fifth. The elephant is either two or four

Depending on the author of the list, and the tiger
Is seven. The lion is three or six. Blue is the
Favorite color of many people because the sky
Is blue and the sea is blue and many people's eyes
Are blue, but blue is not popular in those countries
Where it is the color of mold. In Spain blue
Symbolizes cowardice. In America it symbolizes "Amer-
  icanness."
The racial mixture in North America should
Not be misunderstood. The English came here first,
And the Irish and the Germans and the Dutch. There
  were
Some French here also. The Russians, the Jews, and
The Blacks came afterwards. The women are only
  coming now
To a new kind of prominence in America, where
  "Liberation"
Is their byword. Giraffes, which people ordinarily
Associate with Africa, can be seen in many urban zoos
All over the world. They are an adaptable animal,
As Greek culture was an adaptable culture. Rome
Spread it all over the world. You should know,
Before it did, Alexander spread it as well. Read
As many books as you can without reading interfering
With your time for living. Boxing was formerly illegal
In England, and also, I believe, in America. If
You feel a law is unjust, you may work to change it.
It is not true, as many people say, that
That is just the way things are. Or, Those are the rules,

Immutably. The rules can be changed, although
It may be a slow process. When decorating a window,
  you
Should try to catch the eye of the passer-by, then
Hold it; he or she should become constantly more
Absorbed in what is being seen. Stuffed animal toys
  should be
Fluffy and a pleasure to hold in the hands. They
Should not be too resistant, nor should they be made
With any poisonous materials. Be careful not to set fire
To a friend's house. When covering over
A gas stove with paper or inflammable plastic
So you can paint the kitchen without injuring the stove,
Be sure there is no pilot light, or that it is out.
Do not take pills too quickly when you think you have a
  cold
Or other minor ailment, but wait and see if it
Goes away by itself, as many processes do
Which are really part of something else, not
What we suspected. Raphael's art is no longer as
  popular
As it was fifty years ago, but an aura
Still hangs about it, partly from its former renown.
The numbers seven and eleven are important to remem-
  ber in dice
As are the expressions "hard eight," "Little Joe," and
  "fever,"
Which means *five*. Girls in short skirts when they
Kneel to play dice are beautiful, and even if they
Are not very rich or good rollers, may be

Pleasant as a part of the game. Saint Ursula
And her eleven thousand virgins has
Recently been discovered to be a printer's mistake;
There were only eleven virgins, not eleven thousand.
This makes it necessary to append a brief explanation
When speaking of Apollinaire's parody *Les
Onze Mille Verges*, which means eleven thousand
Male sexual organs—or sticks, for beating. It is a
    pornographic book.
Sexual information should be obtained while one is
    young
Enough to enjoy it. To learn of cunnilingus at fifty
Argues a wasted life. One may be tempted to
Rush out into the streets of Hong Kong or
Wherever one is and try to do too much all in one day.
Birds should never be chased out of a nature sanctuary
And shot. Do not believe the beauty of people's faces
Is a sure indication of virtue. The days of
Allegory are over. The Days of Irony are here.
Irony and Deception. But do not harden your heart.
    Remain
Kind and flexible. Travel a lot. By all means
Go to Greece. Meet persons of various social
Orders. Morocco should be visited by foot,
Siberia by plane. Do not be put off by
Thinking of mortality. You live long enough. There
Would, if you lived longer, never be any new
People. Enjoy the new people you see. Put your hand
    out
And touch that girl's arm. If you are

Able to, have children. When taking pills, be sure
You know what they are. Avoid cholesterol. In conver-
   sation
Be understanding and witty, in order that you may give
Comfort and excitement at the same time. This is the
   high road to popularity
And social success, but it is also good
For your soul and for your sense of yourself. Be
   supportive of others
At the expense of your wit, not otherwise. No
Joke is worth hurting someone deeply. Avoid conta-
   gious diseases.
If you do not have money, you must probably earn
   some
But do it in a way that is pleasant and does
Not take too much time. Painting ridiculous pictures
Is one good way, and giving lectures about yourself is
   another.
I once had the idea of importing tropical birds
From Africa to America, but the test cage of birds
All died on the ship, so I was unable to become
Rich that way. Another scheme I had was
To translate some songs from French into English, but
No one wanted to sing them. Living outside Florence
In February, March, and April was an excellent idea
For me, and may be for you, although I recently
   revisited
The place where I lived, and it is now more "built up";
Still, a little bit further out, it is not, and the fruit trees

18

There seem the most beautiful in the world. Every day
A new flower would appear in the garden, or every other
    day,
And I was able to put all this in what I wrote. I let
The weather and the landscape be narrative in me. To
    make money
By writing, though, was difficult. So I taught
English in a university in spite of my fear that
I knew nothing. Do not let your fear of ignorance keep
    you
From teaching, if that would be good for you, nor
Should you let your need for success interfere with what
    you love,
In fact, to do. Things have a way of working out
Which is nonsensical, and one should try to see
How that process works. If you can understand chance,
You will be lucky, for luck is what chance is about
To become, in a human context, either
Good luck or bad. You should visit places that
Have a lot of savor for you. You should be glad
To be alive. You must try to be as good as you can.
I do not know what virtue is in an absolute way,
But in the particular it is excellence which does not
    harm
The material but ennobles and refines it. So, honesty
Ennobles the heart and harms not the person or the
    coins
He remembers to give back. So, courage ennobles the
    heart

And the bearer's body; and tenderness refines the touch.
The problem of being good and also doing what one
    wishes
Is not as difficult as it seems. It is, however,
Best to get embarked early on one's dearest desires.
Be attentive to your dreams. They are usually about sex,
But they deal with other things as well in an indirect
    fashion
And contain information that you should have.
You should also read poetry. Do not eat too many
    bananas.
In the springtime, plant. In the autumn, harvest.
In the summer and winter, exercise. Do not put
Your finger inside a clam shell or
It may be snapped off by the living clam. Do not wear a
    shirt
More than two times without sending it to the laundry.
Be a bee fancier only if you have a face net. Avoid flies,
Hornets, and wasps. Clasp other people's hands firmly
When you are introduced to them. Say "I am glad to
    meet you!"
Be able to make a mouth and cheeks like a fish. It
Is entertaining. Speaking in accents
Can also entertain people. But do not think
Mainly of being entertaining. Think of your death.
Think of the death of the fish you just imitated. Be
    artistic, and be unfamiliar.
Think of the blue sky, how artists have
Imitated it. Think of your secretest thoughts,

How poets have imitated them. Think of what you feel
Secretly, and how music has imitated that. Make a
　　moue.
Get faucets for every water outlet in your
House. You may like to spend some summers on
An island. Buy woolen material in Scotland and have
The cloth cut in London, lapels made in France.
Become religious when you are tired of everything
Else. As a little old man or woman, die
In a fine and original spirit that is yours alone.
When you are dead, waste, and make room for the
　　future.
Do not make tea from water which is already boiling.
Use the water just as it starts to boil. Otherwise
It will not successfully "draw" the tea, or
The tea will not successfully "draw" it. Byron
Wrote that no man under thirty should ever see
An ugly woman, suggesting desire should be so strong
It affected the princeliest of senses; and Schopenhauer
Suggested the elimination of the human species
As the way to escape from the Will, which he saw as a
　　monstrous
Demon-like force which destroys us. When
Pleasure is mild, you should enjoy it, and
When it is violent, permit it, as far as
You can, to enjoy you. Pain should be
Dealt with as efficiently as possible. To "cure" a dead
　　octopus
You hold it by one leg and bang it against a rock.

This makes a noise heard all around the harbor,
But it is necessary, for otherwise the meat would be too
    tough.
Fowl are best plucked by humans, but machines
Are more humanitarian, since extended chicken
Plucking is an unpleasant job. Do not eat unwashed
    beets
Or rare pork, nor should you gobble uncooked dough.
Fruits, vegetables, and cheese make an excellent diet.
You should understand some science. Electricity
Is fascinating. Do not be defeated by the
Feeling that there is too much for you to know. That
Is a myth of the oppressor. You are
Capable of understanding life. And it is yours alone
And only this time. Someone who excites you
Should be told so, and loved, if you can, but no one
Should be able to shake you so much that you wish to
Give up. The sensations you feel are caused by outside
Phenomena and inside impulses. Whatever you
Experience is both "a person out there" and a dream
As well as unwashed electrons. It is your task to see this
    through
To a conclusion that makes sense to all concerned
And that reflects credit on this poem, your species, and
    yourself.
Now go. You cannot come back until these lessons are
    learned
And you can show that you have learned them for
    yourself.

THE ART OF POETRY

To write a poem, perfect physical condition
Is desirable but not necessary. Keats wrote
In poor health, as did D. H. Lawrence. A combination
Of disease and old age is an impediment to writing, but
Neither is, alone, unless there is arteriosclerosis—that is,
Hardening of the arteries—but that we shall count as a
    disease
Accompanying old age and therefore a negative condi-
    tion.
Mental health is certainly not a necessity for the
Creation of poetic beauty, but a degree of it
Would seem to be, except in rare cases. Schizophrenic
    poetry
Tends to be loose, disjointed, uncritical of itself, in
    some ways

Like what is best in our modern practice of the poetic
    art
But unlike it in others, in its lack of concern
For intensity and nuance. A few great poems
By poets supposed to be "mad" are of course known to
    us all,
Such as those of Christopher Smart, but I wonder how
    crazy they were,
These poets who wrote such contraptions of exigent
    art?
As for Blake's being "crazy," that seems to me very
    unlikely.

But what about Wordsworth? Not crazy, I mean, but
    what about his later work, boring
To the point of inanity, almost, and the destructive
    "corrections" he made
To his *Prelude*, as it nosed along, through the shallows
    of art?
He was really terrible after he wrote the "Ode:
Intimations of Immortality from Recollections of Early
    Childhood," for the most part,
Or so it seems to me. Walt Whitman's "corrections,"
    too, of the *Leaves of Grass*,
And especially "Song of Myself," are almost always
    terrible.

Is there some way to ride to old age and to fame and
    acceptance

And pride in oneself and the knowledge society ap-
    proves one
Without getting lousier and lousier and depleted of
    talent? Yes,
Yeats shows it could be. And Sophocles wrote poetry
    until he was a hundred and one,
Or a hundred, anyway, and drank wine and danced all
    night,
But he was an Ancient Greek and so may not help us
    here. On
The other hand, he may. There is, it would seem, a
    sense
In which one must grow and develop, and yet stay
    young—
Not peroxide, not stupid, not transplanting hair to look
    peppy,
But young in one's heart. And for this it is a good idea
    to have some
Friends who write as well as you do, who know what
    you are doing,
And know when you are doing something wrong.
They should have qualities that you can never have,
To keep you continually striving up an impossible hill.
These friends should supply such competition as will
    make you, at times, very uncomfortable.
And you should take care of your physical body as well
As of your poetic heart, since consecutive hours of
    advanced concentration
Will be precious to your writing and may not be
    possible

If you are exhausted and ill. Sometimes an abnormal or
  sick state
Will be inspiring, and one can allow oneself a certain
  number,
But they should not be the rule. Drinking alcohol is all
  right
If not in excess, and I would doubt that it would be
  beneficial
During composition itself. As for marijuana, there are
  those who
Claim to be able to write well under its influence
But I have yet to see the first evidence for such claims.
Stronger drugs are ludicrously inappropriate, since they
  destroy judgment
And taste, and make one either like or dislike everything
  one does,
Or else turn life into a dream. One does not write well
  in one's sleep.

As for following fashionable literary movements,
It is almost irresistible, and for a while I can see no
  harm in it,
But the sooner you find your own style the better off
  you will be.
Then all "movements" fit into it. You have an "exercy-
  cle" of your own.
Trying out all kinds of styles and imitating poets you
  like
And incorporating anything valuable you may find
  there,

These are sound procedures, and in fact I think even
    essential
To the perfection of an original style which is yours
    alone.
An original style may not last more than four years,
Or even three or even two, sometimes on rare occasions
    one,
And then you must find another. It is conceivable even
    that a style
For a very exigent poet would be for one work only,
After which it would be exhausted, limping, unable to
    sustain any wrong or right.
By "exigent" I mean extremely careful, wanting each
    poem to be a conclusion
Of everything he senses, feels, and knows.
The exigent poet has his satisfactions, which are rela-
    tively special,
But that is not the only kind of poet you can be. There
    is a pleasure in being Venus,
In sending love to everyone, in being Zeus,
In sending thunder to everyone, in being Apollo
And every day sending out light. It is a pleasure to write
    continually
And well, and that is a special poetic dream
Which you may have or you may not. Not all writers
    have it.
Browning once wrote a poem every day of one year
And found it "didn't work out well." But who knows?
He went on for a year—something must have been
    working out.

And why only one poem a day? Why not several? Why
    not one every hour for eight to ten hours a day?
There seems no reason not to try it if you have the
    inclination.

Some poets like "saving up" for poems, others like to
    spend incessantly what they have.
In spending, of course, you get more, there is a
    "bottomless pocket"
Principle involved, since your feelings are changing
    every instant
And the language has millions of words, and the
    number of combinations is infinite.
True, one may feel, perhaps Puritanically, that
One person can only have so much to say, and, besides,
    ten thousand poems per annum
Per person would flood the earth and perhaps eventu-
    ally the universe,
And one would not want so many poems—so there is a
    "quota system"
Secretly, or not so secretly, at work. "If I can write one
    good poem a year,
I am grateful," the noted Poet says, or "six" or "three."
    Well, maybe for that Poet,
But for you, fellow paddler, and for me, perhaps not.
    Besides, I think poems
Are esthetecologically harmless and psychodegradable
And never would they choke the spirits of the world.
    For a poem only affects us

And "exists," really, if it is worth it, and there can't be
    too many of those.
Writing constantly, in any case, is the poetic dream
Diametrically opposed to the "ultimate distillation"
Dream, which is that of the exigent poet. Just how good
    a poem should be
Before one releases it, either from one's own work or
    then into the purview of others,
May be decided by applying the following rules: ask 1)
    Is it astonishing?
Am I pleased each time I read it? Does it say something
    I was unaware of
Before I sat down to write it? and 2) Do I stand up from
    it a better man
Or a wiser, or both? or can the two not be separated? 3)
    Is it really by me
Or have I stolen it from somewhere else? (This some-
    times happens,
Though it is comparatively rare.) 4) Does it reveal
    something about me
I never want anyone to know? 5) Is it sufficiently
    "modern"?
(More about this a little later) 6) Is it in my own
    "voice"?
Along with, of course, the more obvious questions, such
    as
7) Is there any unwanted awkwardness, cheap effects,
    asking illegitimately for attention,
Show-offiness, cuteness, pseudo-profundity, old hat
    checks,

29

Unassimilated dream fragments, or other "literary,"
    "kiss-me-I'm-poetical" junk?
Is my poem free of this? 8) Does it move smoothly and
    swiftly
From excitement to dream and then come flooding
    reason
With purity and soundness and joy? 9) Is this the kind
    of poem
I would envy in another if he could write? 10)
Would I be happy to go to Heaven with this pinned on
    to my
Angelic jacket as an entrance show? Oh, would I? And if
    you can answer to all these Yes
Except for the 4th one, to which the answer should be
    No,
Then you can release it, at least for the time being.
I would look at it again, though, perhaps in two hours,
    then after one or two weeks,
And then a month later, at which time you can
    probably be sure.

To look at a poem again of course causes anxiety
In many cases, but that pain a writer must learn to
    endure,
For without it he will be like a chicken which never
    knows what it is doing
And goes feathering and fluttering through life. When
    one finds the poem
Inadequate, then one must revise, and this can be very
    hard going

Indeed. For the original "inspiration" is not there.
  Some poets never master the
Art of doing this, and remain "minor" or almost
  nothing at all.
Such have my sympathy but not my praise. My sympa-
  thy because
Such work is difficult, and most persons accomplish
  nothing whatsoever
In the course of their lives; at least these poets are
  writing
"First versions," but they can never win the praise
Of a discerning reader until they take hard-hearted
  Revision to bed
And bend her to their will and create through her
  "second-time-around" poems
Or even "third-time-around" ones. There are several
  ways to win
The favors of this lady. One is unstinting labor, but be
  careful
You do not ruin what is already there by unfeeling
  rewriting
That makes it more "logical" but cuts out its heart.
  Unlike the
Sweet, blonde, breasty beauty, Inspiration, Revision is a
  hard-
To-please, mysterious brunette who is won in strange
  ways.
Sometimes neglecting a poem for several weeks is best,
As if you had forgotten you wrote it, and changing it
  then

As swiftly as you can—in that way, you will avoid at
     least dry "re-detailing"
Which is fatal to any art. Sometimes the confidence you
     have from a successful poem
Can help you to find for another one the changes you
     want.
Actually, a night's sleep and a new day filled with
     confidence are very desirable,
And, once you get used to the ordinary pains that go
     with revising,
You may grow to like it very much. It gives one the
     strange feeling
That one is "working on" something, as an engineer
     does, or a pilot
When something goes wrong with the plane; whereas
     the inspired first version of a poem
Is more like simply a lightning flash to the heart.
Revising gives one the feeling of being a builder. And if
     it brings pain? Well,
It sometimes does, and women have pain giving birth to
     children
Yet often wish to do so again, and perhaps the grizzly
     bear has pain
Burrowing down into the ground to sleep all winter. In
     writing
The pain is relatively minor. We need not speak of it
     again
Except in the case of the fear that one has "lost one's
     talent,"

Which I will go into immediately. This fear
Is a perfectly logical fear for poets to have,
And all of them, from time to time, have it. It is very
   rare
For what one does best and that on which one's
   happiness depends
To so large an extent, to be itself dependent on factors
Seemingly beyond one's control. For whence cometh
   Inspiration?
Will she stay in her Bower of Bliss or come to me this
   evening?
Have I gotten too old for her kisses? Will she like that
   boy there rather than me?
Am I a dried-up old hog? Is this then the end of it?
   Haven't I
Lost that sweet easy knack I had last week,
Last month, last year, last decade, which pleased
   everyone
And especially pleased me? I no longer can feel the
   warmth of it—
Oh, I have indeed lost it! Etcetera. And when you write
   a new poem
You like, you forget this anguish, and so on till your
   death,
Which you'll be remembered beyond, not for "keeping
   your talent,"
But for what you wrote, in spite of your worries and
   fears.

The truth is, I think, that one does not lose one's talent,
Although one can misplace it—in attempts to remain in
    the past,
In profitless ventures intended to please those whom
Could one see them clearly one would not wish to
    please,
In opera librettos, or even in one's life
Somewhere. But you can almost always find it, perhaps
    in trying new forms
Or not in form at all but in the (seeming) lack of it—
Write "stream of consciousness." Or, differently again,
    do some translations.
Renounce repeating the successes of the years before.
    Seek
A success of a type undreamed of. Write a poetic fishing
    manual. Try an Art of Love.
Whatever, be on the lookout for what you feared you
    had lost,
The talent you misplaced. The only ways really to lose
    it
Are serious damage to the brain or being so attracted
To something else (such as money, sex, repairing
    expensive engines)
That you forget it completely. In that case, how care
    that it is lost?
In spite of the truth of all this, however, I am aware
That fear of lost talent is a natural part of a poet's
    existence.
So be prepared for it, and do not let it get you down.

Just how much experience a poet should have
To be sure he has enough to be sure he is an adequate
     knower
And feeler and thinker of experience as it exists in our
     time
Is a tough one to answer, and the only sure rule I can
     think of
Is experience as much as you can and write as much as
     you can.
These two can be contradictory. A great many experi-
     ences are worthless
At least as far as poetry is concerned. Whereas the least
     promising,
Seemingly, will throw a whole epic in one's lap.
     However, that is Sarajevo
And not cause. Probably. I do not know what to tell
     you
That would apply to all cases. I would suggest travel
And learning at least one other language (five or six
Could be a distraction). As for sexuality and other
Sensual pleasures, you must work that out for yourself.
You should know the world, men, women, space, wind,
     islands, governments,
The history of art, news of the lost continents, plants,
     evenings,
Mornings, days. But you must also have time to write.
You need environments for your poems and also
     people,
But you also need life, you need to care about these
     things

And these persons, and that is the difficulty, that

What you will find best to write about cannot be
    experienced

Merely as "material." There are some arts one picks up

Of "living sideways," and forwards and backwards at the
    same time,

But they often do not work—or do, to one's disadvan-
    tage:

You feel, "I did not experience that. That cow did

More than I. Or that 'Blue Man' without a thought in
    the world

Beyond existing. He is the one who really exists.

That is true poetry. I am nothing." I suggest waiting a
    few hours

Before coming to such a rash decision and going off

Riding on a camel yourself. For you cannot escape your
    mind

And your strange interest in writing poetry, which will
    make you,

Necessarily, an experiencer and un-experiencer

Of life, at the same time, but you should realize that
    what you do

Is immensely valuable, and difficult, too, in a way riding
    a camel is not,

Though that is valuable too—you two will amaze each
    other,

The Blue Man and you, and that is also a part of life

Which you must catch in your poem. As for how much
    one's poetry

Should "reflect one's experience," I do not think it can avoid

Doing that. The naïve version of such a concern

Of course is stupid, but if you feel the need to "confront"

Something, try it, and see how it goes. To "really find your emotions,"

Write, and keep working at it. Success in the literary world

Is mostly irrelevant but may please you. It is good to have a friend

To help you past the monsters on the way. Becoming famous will not hurt you

Unless you are foolishly overcaptivated and forget

That this too is merely a part of your "experience." For those who make poets famous

In general know nothing about poetry. Remember your obligation is to write,

And, in writing, to be serious without being solemn, fresh without being cold,

To be inclusive without being asinine, particular

Without being picky, feminine without being effeminate,

Masculine without being brutish, human while keeping all the animal graces

You had inside the womb, and beast-like without being inhuman.

Let your language be delectable always, and fresh and true.

Don't be conceited. Let your compassion guide you
And your excitement. And always bring your endeavors
    to their end.

One thing a poem needs is to be complete
In itself and not need others to complement it.
Therefore this poem about writing should be complete
With information about everything concerned in the
    act
Of creating a poem. A work also should not be too long.
Each line should give a gathered new sensation
Of "Oh, now I know that, and want to go on!"
"Measure," which decides how long a poem should be,
Is difficult, because possible elaboration is endless,
As endless as the desire to write, so the decision to end
A poem is generally arbitrary yet must be made
Except in the following two cases: when one embarks
    on an epic
Confident that it will last all one's life,
Or when one deliberately continues it past hope of
    concluding—
Edmund Spenser and Ezra Pound seem examples
Of one of these cases or the other. And no one knows
    how
The Faerie Queene continued (if it did, as one writer
    said,
The last parts destroyed in the sacking of Spenser's
    house
By the crazed but justified Irish, or was it by his
    servants?).

It may be that Spenser never went beyond Book Six
In any serious way, because the thought of ending was
    unpleasant,
Yet his plan for the book, if he wrote on, would oblige
    him to end it. This unlike Pound
Who had no set determined place to cease. Coming to
    a stop
And giving determined form is easiest in drama,
It may be, or in short songs, like "We'll Go
No More a-Roving," one of Byron's most
Touching poems, an absolute success, the best
Short one, I believe, that Byron wrote. In all these
Cases, then, except for "lifetime" poems, there is a
    point one reaches
When one knows that one must come to an end,
And that is the point that must be reached. To reach it,
    however,
One may have to cut out much of what one has written
    along the way,
For the end does not necessarily come of itself
But must be coaxed forth from the material, like a
    blossom.

Anyone who would like to write an epic poem
May wish to have a plot in mind, or at least a
    mood—the
Minimum requirement is a form. Sometimes a stanza,
Like Spenser's, or Ariosto's ottava rima, will set the
    poem going
Downhill and uphill and all around experience

And the world in the maddest way imaginable. Enough,
In this case, to begin, and to let oneself be carried
By the wind of eight (or, in the case of Spenser, nine)
   loud rhymes.
Sometimes blank verse will tempt the amateur
Of endless writing; sometimes a couplet; sometimes
   "free verse."
"Skeltonics" are hard to sustain over an extended
   period
As are, in English, and in Greek for all I know,
   "Sapphics."
The epic has a clear advantage over any sort of lyric
Poem in being there when you go back to it to
   continue. The
Lyric is fleeting, usually caught in one
Breath or not at all (though see what has been said
   before
About revision—it can be done). The epic one is
   writing, however,
Like a great sheep dog is always there
Wagging and waiting to welcome one into the corner
To be petted and sent forth to fetch a narrative bone.
Oh writing an epic! what a pleasure you are
And what an agony! But the pleasure is greater than the
   agony,
And the achievement is the sweetest thing of all. Men
   raise the problem,
"How can one write an epic in the modern world?" One
   can answer,

"Look around you—tell me how one cannot!" Which is
      more or less what
Juvenal said about Satire, but epic is a form
Our international time-space plan cries out for—or so it
      seems
To one observer. The lyric is a necessity too,
And those you may write either alone
Or in the interstices of your epic poem, like flowers
Crannied in the Great Wall of China as it sweeps across
      the earth.
To write only lyrics is to be sad, perhaps,
Or fidgety, or overexcited, too dependent on circum-
      stance—
But there is a way out of that. The lyric must be bent
Into a more operative form, so that
Fragments of being reflect absolutes (see for example
      the verse of
William Carlos Williams or Frank O'Hara), and you
      can go on
Without saying it all every time. If you can master the
      knack of it,
You are a fortunate poet, and a skilled one. You should
      read
A great deal, and be thinking of writing poetry all the
      time.

Total absorption in poetry is one of the finest things in
      existence—
It should not make you feel guilty. Everyone is ab-
      sorbed in something.

41

The sailor is absorbed in the sea. Poetry is the media-
tion of life.

The epic is particularly appropriate to our contempo-
rary world
Because we are so uncertain of everything and also
know too much,
A curious and seemingly contradictory condition, which
the epic salves
By giving us our knowledge and our grasp, with all our
lack of control as well.
The lyric adjusts to us like a butterfly, then epically
eludes our grasp.
Poetic drama in our time seems impossible but actually
exists as
A fabulous possibility just within our reach. To write
drama
One must conceive of an answerer to what one says, as I
am now conceiving of you.

As to whether or not you use rhyme and how "modern"
you are
It is something your genius can decide on every morning
When you get out of bed. What a clear day! Good luck
at it!
Though meter is probably, and rhyme too, probably,
dead
For a while, except in narrative stanzas. You try it out.
The pleasure of the easy inflection between meter and
these easy vocable lines

Is a pleasure, if you are able to have it, you are unlikely
   to renounce.
As for "surrealistic" methods and techniques, they have
   become a
Natural part of writing. Your poetry, if possible, should
   be extended
Somewhat beyond your experience, while still re-
   maining true to it;
Unconscious material should play a luscious part
In what you write, since without the unconscious part
You know very little; and your plainest statements
   should be
Even better than plain. A reader should put your work
   down puzzled,
Distressed, and illuminated, ready to believe
It is curious to be alive. As for your sense of what good
   you
Do by writing, compared to what good statesmen,
   doctors,
Flower salesmen, and missionaries do, perhaps you do
   less
And perhaps more. If you would like to try one of these
Other occupations for a while, try it. I imagine you will
   find
That poetry does something they do not do, whether it
   is
More important or not, and if you like poetry, you will
   like doing that yourself.

Poetry need not be an exclusive occupation.

Some think it should, some think it should not. But you
    should
Have years for poetry, or at least if not years months
At certain points in your life. Weeks, days, and hours
    may not suffice.
Almost any amount of time suffices to be a "minor
    poet"
Once you have mastered a certain amount of the craft
For writing a poem, but I do not see the good of minor
    poetry,
Like going to the Tour d'Argent to get dinner for your
    dog,
Or "almost" being friends with someone, or hanging
    around but not attending a school,
Or being a nurse's aid for the rest of your life after
    getting a degree in medicine,
What is the point of it? And some may wish to write
    songs
And use their talent that way. Others may even end up
    writing ads.
To those of you who are left, when these others have
    departed,
And you are a strange bunch, I alone address these
    words.

It is true that good poetry is difficult to write.
Poetry is an escape from anxiety and a source of it as
    well.
On the whole, it seems to me worthwhile. At the end of
    a poem

One may be tempted to grow too universal, philosophi-
      cal, and vague
Or to bring in History, or the Sea, but one should not
      do that
If one can possibly help it, since it makes
Each thing one writes sound like everything else,
And poetry and life are not like that. Now I have said
      enough.

ON BEAUTY

Beauty is sometimes personified
As a beautiful woman, and this personification is
 satisfying
In that, probably, of all the beautiful things one sees
A beautiful person is the most inspiring, because, in
 looking at her,
One is swept by desires, as the sails are swept in the bay,
 and when the body is excited
Beauty is more evident, whether one is awake or asleep.
A beautiful person also suggests a way
To be at one with beauty, to be united with it,
 physically, with more than our eyes,
And strange it is, this tactile experience
Of beauty, and the subject of many other works. The
 first beauty one sees

That one is conscious of as "beauty," what is that?
Some say
"The mother's face"—but I do not think
The baby is conscious of anything as "beauty"—per-
haps years after
When he looks at Carpaccio's Saint Ursula, he thinks of
"mother"
Subconsciously, and that is why he finds her *bella—*
Poi anche bellissima," as he says in Italian
To the guard or fellow-viewer at his side. The guard
smokes a cigarette
Later, on the steps of the palazzo, and he gazes at the
blue sky,
And for him that is bellissima. Perhaps the sky reminds
him
Of someone's eyes. But why is that, this human
reminder,
If that is what accounts for beauty, so enchanting? Like
a thigh, the island of Kos
Is extremely lovely, as are many other Greek islands—
Lemnos,
Poros, and Charybdis. We could sail among them,
happy, fortunate
To be in such places, yet tormented by an inner sense
Of anxiety and guilt, beleaguered by a feeling we had
torn
Ourselves from what is really important, simply for this
Devious experiencing of "beauty," which may be noth-
ing but a clumsy substitute

47

For seeing our mothers again. But it is not that,
Not a substitute, but something else. There is no going
    backwards in
Pleasure, as Hemingway wrote, in *Death in the After-
    noon*, speaking of Manolete
Who changed the art of bullfighting around, and there
    is
No going backwards, either, in beauty. Mother may still
    be there,
In dimity or in nakedness even, but once you have seen
    Lemnos
It is all over for mother, and Samos and Chios and Kos,
    and
Once you have seen the girls of your own time. Perhaps
    one's earliest experience
Of beauty is a sort of concentrate, with which one
    begins,
And adds the water of a life of one's own; then
Flavors come, and colors, and flowers (if one's
Mother is Japanese, perhaps), mountains covered with
    flowers, and clouds which are the
Colors of blossoming trees. One cannot go back to a
Nightingale in the hope of getting a "more fundamen-
    tal
Experience" of it than one has gotten from Keats's
    poem. This
Schema is not impoverishing but enriching. One does
Not have the Ode instead of the bird, one has them
    both. And so

48

With mother (although mother dies), and so with the
    people
We love, and with the other things of this world. What,
    in
Fact, is probably the case is that the thigh
And nose and forehead of a person have an interchange-
    able
Relationship with landscape; we see
The person first: as babies we aren't tourists, and our
    new-flung eyes
Are not accustomed to looking at mountains, although
Soon we see breasts—and later see the Catskills, the
Berkshires and the Alps. And as we were moved by
    breasts before
We are moved by mountains now. Does that mean the
World is for us to eat? that our lives are a constant re-
Gression? Or "Plato inside out"? Or might it not mean,
    as
I have suggested, that we are born to love either or
    both?

Beautiful, Charybdis, are your arms, and beautiful your
    hands;
Beautiful in the clear blue water are the swift white-
    tinted waves;
Beautiful is the "starlight" (is there any light there,
Really? We may come to the question in a while of
    whether
Beauty is a reflection); beautiful is the copy

49

Of Michelangelo's David, and the original; beautiful
    the regatta
Of happy days one receives, and beautiful the haymow
From which the birds have just flown away. If they
Have left some eggs there, let us go and look at them
To see if they are beautiful as well.

If all these things are carry-overs from mother,
Then mother is everywhere, she completes our con-
    sciousness
On every side and of every sight we see. We thank you,
    mother,
If that is so, and we will leave you there at the beginning
    of it all, with dad.

It is always a possibility that beauty does not exist
In the realest sense, but that is just as true of everything
    else,
So in a way it does not modify this poem but actually
    strengthens it
By being a part of the awareness that puts it together.

Beauty suggests endlessness and timelessness, but
    beauty
Is fleeting in individual instances, though a person's
Or a landscape's beauty may last for quite a long while.
It is worth preserving, by exercise, good diet, and other
Ways of keeping in good health, and in the case of
Landscape, careful gardening, and good, enforceable
    zoning and

Anti-pollution laws. Even though it may cause despera-
tion
In the abstract, the thought that "beauty is only for a
day,"
So to speak, in individual instances it need not. A good
Night's sleep and wake up happy at all that is beautiful
now
Is the best remedy. It is just a quality of beauty that
It comes and it goes. We are contented with the ocean's
Being that way, and summer, winter, fall, and
Spring also leave and return. If beauty does not return
In all cases to the same objects, we must simply be alert
and
Find it where it has gone. Every good artist knows
This, and every person should know it as well, it being
One thing one can learn from art, and of course as I said
From close study of nature—though art is sometimes
easier
To learn from, whether one is viewing it or creating it.
People, of course, are often depressed,
Despite philosophy and art, about the loss of their own
Beauty, and it is a fact that once one has something
To no longer have it is a sorrow, and there is nothing
This poem can do about that. On the other hand,
You participated in it for a while (for twenty or for
Forty years) and that is pretty good. And there it is,
Shining in the world. Your own exterior is, after
All, just a tiny part of that.

Beauty quite naturally seems as if it would be beautiful

No matter how we looked at it, but this is not always
   true. Take a microscope to
Many varieties of beauty and they are gone. A young
   girl's
Lovely complexion, for example, reveals gigantic pores,
   hideously, gapingly
Embedded in her, as Gulliver among the Brobdingna-
   gians observed. And
Put some of her golden hair under the microscope:
   huge,
Portentous, menacing tubes. But since
Our eyes aren't microscopic, who cares? To have an
Operation to make them so would be insane. A certain
Sanity is necessary for life, and even our deepest studies
   need not
Carry us beyond a certain place, i.e. right here, the place
Where we would get microscopic eyes. Nor is it
   necessary to
Pluck out the eyes of an animal (a dog, say) and
Transplant them for our own, so we can see
Beauty as a dog sees it, or as a kangaroo or as a
   rhinoceros.
We do not know if animals see beauty at all, or if
They merely see convenience and sex, a certain useful
   log here or there a
Loyalty-retaining moving creature. I do not think we
   need to know,
Physically, in our own bodies. To give up our human
   eyes,

And indeed our human brain, for those of a horse or
  lion might
Be fantastic to write a book about, but then we would
Never know anything else. I suggest, instead,
Walking around beautiful objects, if one can, for that
Is sometimes very pleasant and reveals newer and, if
That is possible, even more beautiful views. One's first
  view
Of the Bay of Baia, for example, may be improved
Sharply by the view from a boat coming into the harbor
  or
From the Hotel Shamrock on the mountain's peak.
  First sight of a girl
Is often one of best ones, but later, sighing above her in
  bed,
She is even more beautiful. And then in a.m. waking
  you up
With a happy alarm. Who would want microscopic eyes
  at
Such a moment? or macroscopic ones, for that matter,
  which would make
Your girl look extremely tiny, almost invisible, like an
  insect
You might swat, if you weren't careful; and you would
  feel
Funny, wondering how someone so small
Could make you feel so happy; and it would be so
  hallucinatory, to
Go to bed with her and hold her in your arms, for unless
  you had

Macrotactile arm and hand nerves as well, she would
Feel as large as you are, almost, and yet be so small!
    You
Would think you were stoned on something monstrous.
    I think
The proportion between eye and nature, then, is, as
Far as beauty goes, the most important proportion of
    all.

Like your own eyes, it is probably best to accept your
    own culture
In responding to what is beautiful. To try to transform
    yourself
To an Ancient Mesopotamian or a Navajo priest
In order to decide on the beauty of a stallion or a
Stone jar could end up being an impediment to actually
    seeing anything. Some
Knowledge is helpful, but you should exercise reason
    and control.

In general, any sort of artificial aids
To looking at something may be an impediment to
    beauty
Unless you are so thoroughly accustomed to them that
You do not know they are there. So a telescope,
When looking at the Valley of the Arno for the first
    time, may not
Give the pleasure you might get from your naked eye,
Even if your eye did not enable you to see things in
So much detail. Eyeglasses can be annoying at first, as

People are right to look for a beautiful mate and to
Put windows where the beauty is outside.

Animals, though natural and strange, I do not usually
    find beautiful,
Or fish or insects either. I do not know why this is.
    Many
People feel otherwise. Birds make me think uncomfor-
    tably of color
(Except when they whiz past by surprise) and the idea
    of feathers
I find disturbing. Whatever its cause, a strong feeling of
    discomfort
Makes hard the perception of beauty. You should not
    worry
If some people find some things beautiful that you do
    not
Find so. There is probably something that seems ugly to
    others
Which gives you the pleasure that beauty brings
Into our lives. Such strong feelings as physical
Discomfort, or deprivation, or a terror of disease or
Death, can make beauty unlikely to get through to you.
    It may be
That seeing birds in a more natural, everyday way would
Make them seem more beautiful to me. I do not know
Since this has not happened. Birds are something I was
    told
Were "beautiful" when I was a child. Flowers also were,
    and

Especially roses. I am still slightly uncomfortable with
Roses. The moon and the stars were also on my parents'
    and
Teachers' list of what was beautiful. It has been
Hard for me to love them (stars and moon, I mean) but
    I have,
Despite this early "training," which may be injurious to
    beauty
In some cases, in others not. In raising your child,
You should share your feeling with him of what is
    beautiful,
But do not expect a child to respond to it that way.
He or she is likely to respond more like a poet or an
    artist,
By wanting to "do" something with it—to run
Through it, or eat it or tear it apart. It is in later life
    perhaps
Precisely the suppression of these feelings, or some of
    these feelings,
That results in our feeling of beauty, which we are
    merely to contemplate.
Contemplation seemed to Aristotle the superior mode,
    to others may seem an unnatural mode
Of life. Most people still feel in the presence of beauty
    that old wish
To do something, whether it is to make love
To the beautiful person, in the case it is a person, or if
It is a landscape or a seemingly billion stars, or a
Light blue scarcely rippling bay, to run through it, get
    out a

Telescope, or dive in and swim or build a boat or buy a
    piece of
Property adjoining it. Sometimes it is merely an impulse
    to
Jump up and down, or to scream, or to call people up
    on the telephone to
Tell them about what one has seen. In any case,
    nothing satisfies
The impulse but merely exhausts it. The perception of
    beauty wears out
After a while, speeded up by activity, and then one is all
    right again or
Not all right again, depending on how you look at it.
    Remembered beauty,
On the other hand, if protected properly, can be a
    source of light and
Heat to one's imagination and one's sense of life, like
The sun shining in on one's shoulder. It is difficult to
    make
The impression of beauty last as it is difficult to make
    the pleasure of love-
Making last for days, but it can sometimes happen. The
    length of time one stays with
Something one thinks is beautiful can help it to stay
With one, so going back through the gallery is often a
    good idea.
In these cases, contemplation itself is a form of activity
The object of beauty incites. But children, told to
    contemplate
In this way, are likely to dislike what they see

Because they cannot contemplate and thus can do
    nothing
With it. Beauty, along with seeming strange, natural,
    and being temporal
And adapted to the size of human eyes and being a
    concentrate
With time added, must also seem like something of
    one's own.
Roses and birds belonged to my mother and her friends.
    I loved
Tulips, daisies, daffodils, and the white
Tiny flowers whose name I don't know which grew in
The woods in back of my house, which was used as a
    dump (the
Woods, I mean) and which were so small they were
    useless for the decoration of homes.

One reaction beauty sometimes causes, in the absence
Of other responses, is that it makes one cry, perhaps
Because of seeming a possibility of happiness projected
Into the past, as it is, in fact, in space, which one
Can never again reach, because irrevocably behind one.
    It may be
That there was never any chance of the kind of
    happiness
Beauty suggests, and thus that our tears are
In vain, but it is hard to imagine what "useful" tears
    would be
After one is an adult. Crying is crying, and
Blossoming plum and cherry trees may make one cry

A good deal, as may rocky coastlines and Renaissance
art.
The tears in such cases are probably caused by the
conflict
Beauty sends up of "Too much! There is no way to
Deal with me!" And the presence of beauty may make
Tears easier and seem safer, too, since it seems, also, to
warrant and protect.

If none of the actions we take in regard to beauty
Seems completely satisfactory, and if we go on feeling
An impulse to do, to finally do something when we are
in its presence, then
It may be either that beauty is a front for something
else or that
It has a purpose our minds have not penetrated yet—or
both. Many people
Say that it is all a trick of "Nature." "Nature" makes
people
Beautiful, so people will make love to each other and
the
Human race will go on, which "Nature" apparently
desires.
Others, and sometimes some of these same ones,
assume there is
A God, a Divine Being, with absolute power, who also
wishes
The human race to go on, as well as to remind them
By the beauty of mountains, lakes, and trees (as well as
of human features)

Of how bountiful He is, so that they will do His Will.
   The
Human features are lovely, also, to remind them
Of what God Himself looks like (approximately). I
   believe
All this is too simple to be correct, but you are free to
   believe what you will.
Nor can I subscribe to the "Analogy Theory" of beauty,
That beautiful things exist to show us how to behave
To ourselves and to each other. For one thing, the
   correspondence
Is insufficiently clear—just how that blue sky, for
   example, can
Help me to do what is right. It is true that clarity and
   harmony
May be the result of an ethical action, but it is also
True, often, that such actions involve pain and depriva-
   tion
Which seem inimical to beauty, and which I cannot see
   up there at all.

The beauty of many things does seem to show
They are good for us (or good for our descendants), but
What about poison flowers and berries? Treacherous
   bays? Beautiful.
Wolf women who simply wish to devour us? What
   about Blake's Tyger?
My own view is that we are in a situation
That is not under our control (or anyone's, for that
   matter) but

Which we can handle, if we are wise about it, fairly
    well.
Temper your admiration for beauty with whatever
Else you know of the particular example you are
    looking at. Do not
Leap into a reflection in a lake, or take up with a bad
    woman
Because her breasts are beautiful, or commit
Suicide because Botticelli's *Venus* (it is not a real
Situation) reminds you of what your life has not been.
    These are times to let the
"Enchantment" wear off for a while—for it is an
Enchantment, and it will go away. You will feel driven
To act on your feeling immediately, and—
Perhaps you should go ahead and do it, even though
    you will be destroyed.
Not every man can die for beauty. Perhaps there is
    some kind of List
On which your name will be recorded. I don't know. I
    don't know if I approve of that.
However, my approval may not be that which you are
    after.
As a young man myself I felt I would do anything for
Beauty, but actually I was fairly cautious and did
Nothing that seemed likely to result in the destruction
    of my ability
To stay around and have these ideas and put them into
    words.
I would go forward one step, and back another, in
    regard to

Beauty, but beauty of course was mingled with other
   things. I don't
Propose myself as a model. Far from that. Since I am
   still the
Same way, I am interested, though, in if how I am
Makes sense to me in the light of these other things I
   am saying.

One thing I notice I have done which does seem right to
   me
Is to think about beauty a good deal and see many
   examples
Of it, which has helped me to have what is called "good
   taste"
In it, so I am able to enjoy a great many things
That I otherwise could not have. Discriminating taste
   does not
Decrease the amount of beauty you perceive, but adds
   to it.
If you notice an opposite effect, you are "improving" in
The wrong way. Go visit a lot of foreign places
Where ordinary things have an extraordinary aspect and
   thus
Invite you to see them esthetically. Travel with some-
   one
Else, and travel alone. Stand in front of a beautiful
   object until you
Are just about to feel tired of being there, then stop
And turn away. Vary your experience of what you see.

In variety is refreshment of the senses. A great paint-
ing, a
Mountain, and a person are a good combination for
one day.
Sometimes, sameness increases beauty, or, rather,
Variety within sameness, as when looking at beautiful
twins,
Triplets, or quadruplets, or in climbing a lot of stair-
cases in Genoa,
A city famed for the beautiful structure of its stairways.

The impulse to "do something" about beauty
Can be acted on, as we have seen, by making love or,
sometimes,
Even by marrying. Man is capable of improving
The beauty of nature in numerous ways, of which
planting
Huge long rows of beautiful flowers is not the least. The
Cannas are nodding, the roses are asleep. And here's a
Tiny or medium-sized bumblebee, no it's a great big
one!
And the oleanders are planted, they are standing
Next to the palms. You feel a surge of unaccountable
delight. The wind moves them. And
Extraordinary cities may also be tucked together by
Human imaginations and hands. And other works of art
as well.

Beauty is perceived in a curious way in poems,

Like the ocean seen through a partially knocked-down
  wall.
In music, beauty is "engaged in," as in sculpture and
  dance.

"I am beautiful, O mortals, like a dream of stone." says
Beauty, in Baudelaire's sonnet "La Beauté," where
  Baudelaire, in
Fewer words than I, has set down his ideas on the
  subject. Essentially he
Sees Beauty as eternal and pure, an enslaver of poets.
Rilke says that we love beauty because it "so serenely
Disdains to destroy us." In making works of art, then,
Is the excitement we feel that of being close to the
  elements of
Destruction? I do not want any mystery in this poem, so
  I will
Let that go. Or, rather, I want the mystery to be that it
  is clear
But says nothing which will satisfy completely but
  instead stirs to action (or contemplation)
As beauty does—that is, I wish it to be beautiful. But
  why I want that,
Even, I do not entirely know. Well, it would put it in a
  class of things
That seems the highest, and for one lifetime that should
  be enough.

Beauty is sometimes spoken of
As if it were a "special occasion," like going to the ballet

If one does that only once a year, or like going to
Church, if one does that only on religious holidays. Ex-
Perienced in this peripheral fashion, beauty cannot be
Sufficiently understood so as to be as valuable
To us as it should be, even if we do not understand it
Completely. Some understanding will rub off from
    frequent
Contact with it in both physical and intellectual ways,
And this understanding will do us some good. Of
    course,
It is possible to live without ever having seen mountains
Or the ocean, but it is not possible to live without
    having seen some
Beauty, and once one has seen something and
Liked it, one wants to have something more to do with
It, even to the point of having it inextricably tangled
Up with one's life, which beauty may be, anyway,
    whether we
Want it to be or not. It is a pleasure to be on top of
    things,
Even if only for a moment. Beauty may be an unsatisfia-
    ble
Appetite inducer, the clue to an infinite mystery, or a
    hoax,
Or perhaps a simple luxury for those with enough
    money and time
To go in pursuit of it, like châteaux vintages. Or it may
    be the whole works (see
Keats). It may simply be a bloom which is followed by

Fruition and not supposed to last and we have per-
    versely arranged things
So in many cases it does, the way we force-feed geese
And pigs, and now we are simply stuck with it, grunting
    and
Cackling all around us, from which we try to make
    music.
Or it may be that beauty is an invitation
To a party that doesn't exist (Whitman thinks the party
    exists).
In any case, you will probably want as much
Of it as you can take with you, because it is, in spite of
All the doubts expressed above, certainly one of the
    sweetest things
In life. Of course, this is not the end of the subject, but
    it is
As far as I now can see, which in regard to beauty is
All we have, and one thing it seems to be about.

THE ART OF LOVE

"What do you know about it?"

1

To win the love of women one should first discover
What sort of thing is likely to move them, what feelings
They are most delighted with their lives to have;
    then
One should find these things and cause these feelings.
    Now
A story illustrates: of course the difficulty
Is how to talk about winning the love
Of women and not also speak of loving—a new
Problem? an old problem? Whatever—it is a something
    secret
To no one who has finally experienced it. Presbyopic.
    And so,
Little parks in Paris, proceed, pronounce
On these contributing factors to the "mental psyche

Of an airplane." Renumerate
The forces which gloss our tongues! And then, Betty,
The youngest rabbit, ran, startled, out into the drive-
    way,
Fear that Terry will run over her now calmed. Back
To the Alps, back to the love of women, the sunset
Over "four evenly distributed band lots in
Which you held my hand," mysterious companion
With opal eyes and oval face without whom I
Could never have sustained the Frogonian evening—
Wait a minute! if this is to be a manual of love, isn't it
Just about time we began? Well . . . yes. Begin.

Tie your girl's hands behind her back and encourage her
To attempt to get loose. This will make her breasts look
Especially pretty, like the Parthenon at night. Some-
    times those illuminations
Are very beautiful, though sometimes the words
Are too expected, too French, too banal. Ain't youse a
    cracker,
Though? And other poems. Or Freemasonry Revisited.
    Anyway,
Tie her up. In this fashion, she will be like Minnie
    Mouse, will look
Like starlight over the sensuous Aegean. She will be the
    greatest thing you ever saw.
However, a word of advice, for cold September eve-
    nings,
And in spring, summer, winter too, and later in the fall:

Be sure she likes it. Or only at first dislikes it a little bit.
    Otherwise
You are liable to lose your chances for other kinds of
    experiments,
Like the Theseion, for example. Or the two-part song.
    Yes! this
Is Athens, king of the cities, and land of the
Countries of the Fall. Where *atoma* means person, and
    where was
A lovely epoch once though we however must go on
With contemporary problems in ecstasy. Let's see. Your
Girl's now a little tied up. Her hands stretched behind
    her at
An angle of about 40 degrees to her back, no, say,
    seventeen
And Z——sending his first roses at seventeen (roses also
    work
As well as hand tying but in a different less fractured
Framework) and she receiving them writing "I have
    never
Received roses before from a man. Meet me at the
    fountain
At nine o'clock and I will do anything you want." He
    was
Panicky! and didn't know what to do. What had he
    wanted
That now seemed so impossible? he didn't exactly know
How to do it. So he wrote to her that night amid the
    capitals

Of an arboring civilization, "Fanny I can't come. The
    maid is shocked. The
Butter factory is in an endzone of private feelings. So
The chocolate wasp stands on the Venetian steps. So
The cloudbursts are weeping, full of feeling
And stones, so the flying boats are loving and the tea
Is full of quotients. So—" That's enough cries Fanny
    she tears
It up then she reads it again. One breast may be
    somewhat higher
Than another with the hands tied behind. As Saint
    Ursula and her Virgins
Had the right attitude but were in the wrong field of
    fancy,
Not the sexual field, so these erogenous zones come
Forward when we need them if we are lucky and now I
    will speak
Of the various different virtues of rope, string, and
    chicken-wire—
If you want her to break loose suddenly in the middle
Of the lovemaking episode when you are inside her and
    cry yes
Yes throwing her arms and hands around you, then try
    string. Otherwise rope is most practical. As at
    Ravenna
The mosaics that start from the wall stay on the wall, in
The wall and they are the wall, in a sense, like the tracks
    in Ohio,
Pennsylvania, and Illinois. Rounding the bend you will
    see them.

They are hard to tell from the earth. She will kiss you
   then.

Thank you, parents of loving and passive girls, even a
   little bit masochistic ones
Who like the things this book is recommending. It is to
   you,
Although they do not know you often and
Even if they did might not consider this, men owe these
   joys.

To lack a woman, to not have one, and to be longing
   for one
As the grass grows around the Perrier family home
That is the worst thing in life, but nowhere near the
   best is to have one
And not know what to do. So we continue these
   instructions.

The woman's feet may be tied as well as her hands. I'd
   suggest tying them
Or really the ankles, that's easier, to the legs at the foot
   of the bed
Or of the pool table if that is what you are making love
   upon. I
Remember a day in Paris when a man had a dancing bear
And I walked home to Freesia thinking about ape-mon-
   gering and death—Hold on a minute, there are
White blocks or cubes on the jetty of French poetic-po-
   litical involvement

73

Which "Love Does Not Need a Home" will cannily
     play for you on the phonograph
If you are not AC/DC ruining a certain part of the
     equipment. Her smile
Will be glorious, a sunrise, her feet tied to the legs of
     the bed.
If her hands are free she can move up and down readily
     (the
Sit up/lie down movement, near the Boulevard Raspail
And in irregular patterns—for some reason certain
     details
Keep coming back to undermine their candidacies).
     What good this will be to you
I don't know, but her sitting up and then lying down
     will (again)
Make her breasts look pretty (Fontainebleau you are
     my ark,
And Issy you are my loom!) and give tensity to the
     throat
Muscles and the stomach muscles too! You can simply
     enjoy that
(The tensing in the abdomen) by putting, lightly, your
     fingers on it (the
Abdomen) as one voyages on a Sunday to the Flea
     Market
Not in the hope of really finding anything but of
     sensing a new light panorama of one's needs.
So much for the pleasure in tensing stomach muscles.
     Of course with the girl tied this way

You can hit her up and down if you like to do that
And she will never be able to get up and walk away
Since she can't walk without her feet, and they are tied
     to the bed.

If you combine tying her hands to the bed and her feet
You can jump on her! She will be all flattened and
     splayed out.
What a fine way to spend an autumn afternoon, or an
     April one!
So delicious, you jumping up and down, she lying there,
     helpless, enjoying your every gasp!
You may enter her body at this point of course as well
As the Postal Museum stands only a few meterage yards
     away.
They have a new stamp there now, of a king with his
     crown
On backwards, dark red, it is a mistake, and worth five
     million pounds!
You can come out and go there, away! Dear, stay with
     me!!
And she pleads with you there as she lies on the bed,
     attached to the bed
By the cords you have tied with your hands, and
     attached to you by her love
As well, since you are the man who attached her there,
Since you are the knowing lover using information
     gleaned from this volume.

Tying up, bouquets, bouqueting bunch-of-flowers
    effects. Tie her hands and legs
Together, I mean her hands and feet, I mean ankles.
    There are different processes.
Tie the left hand to the left ankle, right hand to right
    ankle.
Spread out in any position and make love. She will be
    capable of fewer movements
But may bring you a deep-sea joy. Crabs and lobsters
    must love like that
And they don't stay down at the bottom of the ocean
    for nothing—
It must be wonderful! In any case you can try it in your
    mistress's bed
Or in your own course. You can tie left hand to right
    ankle
And so on. This gives a criss-cross effect
And is good after a quarrel. The breasts in all these
    cases look
Exceptionally beautiful. If you do not like liking
These breasts so much you may hit them
If she likes that, and ask her to ask you to hit them,
    which
Should increase your pleasure in mastery particularly if
    she is all tied up.
"Hit My Tits" could be a motto on the sailboat of your
    happiness. If you don't think
You have gotten your money's worth already
From this book you deserve to turn in an early grave
Surrounded by worm women who assail and hit you

76

Until there is nothing left of you so hard that they can't
   eat.
But I am sure this is not your feeling. So, having agreed,
Let us go on. You should buy another book
And give it to your best friend, however, if at this point
   you do agree with me.
I will wait; meanwhile we can both stare at your
   mistress, where she is all tied up.

Well, you can roll her like a wheel, though I doubt
   she'll approve of it,
Women rarely do, I knew one once, though, who did.
   For
This of course you use the right hand right ankle left
Hand left ankle arrangement, using splints on both sides
   of each
Knot so that the limbs will stay in wheel-position. Now
   that she
Looks like that which makes a chariot roll, roll her! If
   this hurts her,
Soothe her a little by kissing her all around, saying
"Ah, my lovely wheel, went over a bump, did it?" and so
   on,
Until she finally is resigned to being your wheel, your
   dear beloved one
And is eager to be rolled about by you. Small objects
   placed on the floor
Will give you brief twinges of sadistic energy and speed
   up your wheeling.
I suggest ending by wheeling her out an opened door

77

Which you then close and stab yourself to death. This
  procedure, however, is rare.
I was carried away. Forgive me. The next chapters will
  be much more sane.

Nailing a woman to the wall causes too much damage
(Not to the wall but to the woman—you after all want
  to enjoy her
And love her again and again). You can, however, wrap
  tape around her arms, waist, ankles, and knees
And nail this to the wall. You'll enjoy the pleasure of
  nailing
And the very thought of it should make her scream. You
  can fit this tape
On her like tabs, so your girl will be like a paper doll.
And you can try things on her once she is nailed up.
  You can also
Throw things at her, which is something I very much
  like to do—
Small rakes, postal scales, aluminum belt buckles,
  Venetian glass clowns—
As soon as you start to hurt her, you should stop
And kiss her bruises, make much of them, draw a circle
  around each hit
With a bold felt pen. In this way you can try to hit the
  same spots over and over again
As the little park grows larger the more you look at it
But the flowers are in another story, a lemon-covered
  volume, stop! The knees

Of this girl are now looking very pretty, so go and kiss
them
And slip your hands around the back of them and feel
what is called
The inside of the knee and tell her you love her.
If she is able to talk she will probably ask you to take
her down,
Which you then can do. However, if she wants to stay
up there
As blue day changes to night, and is black in the
hemispheres, and boats go past
And you are still feeling wonderful because of her
beautiful eyes
And breasts and legs, leave her there and run up against
her
As hard as you can, until the very force of your bumping
Breaks tape from nail or girl from tape or breaks great
chunks of wall
So you and she lie tumbled there together
Bruises on her body, plaster on your shoulders, she
bloody, she hysterical, but joy in both your hearts.
Then pull off the tape if it hasn't come off
And bite her to the bone. If she bites you back, appoint
her
"Lover" for a while and let her do all this to you. That
is,
If you'd like it. You'll suffer, of course, from being less
beautiful than she
And less soft, less inviting to cause pain to. To be a
great lover,

However, you must be a great actor, so try, at least
    once.

Oh the animals moving in the stockyards have no idea
    of these joys
Nor do the birds flying high in the clouds. Think:
    tenderness cannot be all
Although everyone loves tenderness. Nor violence,
    which gives the sense of life
With its dramas and its actions as it is. Making love
    must be everything—
A city, not a street; a country, not a city; the universe,
    the world—
Make yours so, make it even a galaxy, and be conscious
    and unconscious of it all. That is the art of love.

2

Which cannot be begun, however, until you meet
    somebody
You want to make love to, a subject to be dealt with in
    these chapters.
So, avanti! Here you are, girl-less, wandering the city's
    streets
Or deep in the country, pale amid flowers, or staring,
    perhaps too!,

At barrels of camel dung being shoved down a road in
the Middle East
Or on a skyscraper in a great city, ten thousand miles
beneath the ocean floor,
How do you meet a woman? or, if you like younger
women, a girl?
Well, the thing to do is find out where local girls
congregate—
This may be at the camel shack, along the shore of the
Ashkenazi or the Mediterranean
At a beach, or along the side streets or at the school,
wherever
It is, go there! You will be happy once you have seen
the girls
Or women and your body becomes active, reminding
you you must succeed
As the earthquake and the volcano remind life they
must succeed
And it must succeed. Success is a joy although it is not
everything,
Still, in matters of love, there is nothing without it!
With no
Success, simply nothing happens. You are a dead person
in a field
With mud being heaped on you; without success,
Nothing happens in the field of love. Something
Has to be there, a spark, a firm handclasp, a meaningful
look, some hope,
Something, which one only can get in the presence of
women

Since if they are not there, how can they give it? But
You do not need to be reminded of this, you are already
    reading
This strangely eventful and staggering "Art of Love."

Many people get married before they even realize how
    to meet girls
And so have a wide selection; this may result in
    infidelity, divorce,
And frustrated feelings; so it is a good idea, whether you
    are contemplating marriage or not,
To learn where to meet, to find the women whom you
    might love.
In big cities often guidebooks are accurate indications
Of some of the spots to begin your search. Great tourist
    attractions
Such as the Acropolis, the Bermuda Shorts factory, and
    St. Peters in Rome
Are likely to attract women as well as men, since they
    too share such human feelings
As curiosity, interest, the desire to find "something afar
From the sphere of our sorrow" (as Shelley says), always
    hoping to find this,
Even as men are, in some storied successes of history,
    business, or art.
So that is a good place to meet them, too, since their
    souls are likely to be open
In a way they are not otherwise: historical beauty is a
    friend,

Opening and softening the feelings, but no human
    friend is there,
So you may fill the gap by sharing the openness with
    her,
And by appreciating the work at hand. Some like to fall
    down right there
And "made love my first sight of the Acropolis" or
"Bellini's pictures moved me, so—" As the ferry boat
Pursues its course from Brindisi to Corfu and back again
Many young couples were seen steaming on its decks
With happy energy, and among the lime trees in
    Southern Africa
A thousand hippopotamuses met with glee and fright-
    ened everyone away
By their lovemaking, which increased the acidity of the
    limes
One million per cent. Why should they be having all
    the fulfilment and fun
And you not? My friends, there is no reason. So another
    kind of place to go
In cities is the college restaurants. There young girls
    congregate speaking of their courses
And their boyfriends and their professors. You can
    pretend to be a poet
Or a professor, and speak to them about starting a little
    shop
Where no one will come. Their curiosity piqued, they
    may follow you as far as a coffee shop
Where you can go on speaking to them, in private—but
    that is covered in

83

The next chapter—"Antic," or "What to Say." Some-
   times a department store
Will be full of women. You can go as a woman yourself,
   as a
Cripple who needs their help, or as a regular man
   shopping for some real woman he knows
Who needs their advice. It doesn't matter how you go;
   what matters
Is getting the woman alone, so you can speak of your
   desires.
No one can resist this, but first you have to find the one
   to speak to.
Well, almost no one—but your ratio anyway should be
   seven to one,
Success over failure. Dangerous intersections in mid-city
Are good places to meet girls and help them across the
   street.
You can stand there and do this all day, madly dodging
   the traffic
And with a happy smile you find the one you like and
   cross her too
With a swift hit on the belly and a large and wicked
   smile.
She will look at you surprised and you can carry on from
   there, but at least you will be beginning
With her grateful to you, for having steered her across
   the street.

Life is full of horrors and hormones and so few things
   are certain,

So many unknown—but the pleasure of coupling with a
    creature one is crazy about
Is something undisputed. So don't be afraid to spend
Hours, even days, weeks, even months, going to places
And trying to find the person who can give you the
    maximum pleasure in life
As the sun hits the top of mountains but often prefers
    the hills
Where markets glint in the fading light and one's lungs
    seem filled with silver. O horrors of loneliness!
Abandon my spirit while it walks forth through the
    world and attempts to find for people
And tell them where marvelous women can be found.
    Of course, you want a very particular one.
To find her, however, you may have to look at a great
    many, and try more,
Some in the light, some in the dark. Orgies are
    sometimes organized for people,
You can try that, but I wouldn't, all life is an
Orgy, why limit oneself to a little room, full of
    (probably)
Mainly people who are emotionally disturbed
As you and I are not. If you could organize an orgy
Of your own, that might, I think, be something else.
    But
We have strayed from our subject. The Cross of the
    Seven Winds Hotel
On East Vortex Street, in Albenport, is a good place to
    meet girls,

It so happens there are always a tremendous number of
   them there
And no one has ever known why. But you know what
   custom is (or fashion). It's a great place to go.
If you can't find it, take some girl you already have
And like (if you have one) and whip her until she tells
   you where it is (most women know).
If she hasn't replied after ten strokes it's a sign she loves
   you
So dearly and is so jealous she is willing to undergo pain
   for you,
Set sail with her for Zhak or Brindisi right away, she is
   the one to love you
For the rest of your life and you will only need this
   manual
In its earlier and later parts, not this part, you already
   have your girl.

Happy the man who has two breasts to crush against his
   bosom,
A tongue to suck on, a lip to bite, and in fact an entire
   girl! He knows a success
Not known by Mount Aetna or Vesuvius or by any
   major volcano of the world!
He has someone to come into, and stay there, and
   tremble, and shake about, and hold,
And dream about, and come back to, and even discuss
   party politics with if he wants to,
Or poetry, or painting. But where shall you find this
   bird? On a gondola in Venice

The tour guide said, "Look at those buildings" and I
    felt my chest crushed against your
Bosom, and the whole earth went black; when I awoke
    we were in Brindisi,
You had nailed me to a canoe, you were standing on my
    stomach, you had a rat in your hand
Which you were waving in the summer breeze, and
    saying "This is from the Almanach
Of Living, attention, please pay attention, greeniness
    and mountains, oh this is the art of love!"

Uncooperative cities! your hideous buildings block out
    air and sunlight! Fumes
Destroy human lungs! Muggers and burglars
Infest your streets! You're horrible! I hate you! (Some-
    times.) Where else are women to be found
And the sweet joys they furnish, the prospect of a life
    joined to a life
More wonderful than air joined to a fountain—there is
    nothing like the art of love!
A plume, a cabana, a canvas, a modern tire, a pampa, a
    plume, a sailboat
All have meaning as an ocean has tar, in relation to love
    only. Yes,
That's my secret. What is yours? I mean to say without
    love everything is only half in order,
Or two-fifths, or one-third, perhaps for many and I think
    I am one
Hardly ordered at all, for us, without love, life is a great
    mess! By order I mean clarity, I mean joy.

In India the art of love has been studied in great detail
But that was in another age, another time. My book
    brings it all up to date
And is oriented to the Western World! Though my
    Chinese edition
May soon be out! Here's just a hint of it: "Think in
    love,
Don't think in rabbits." But now back to the Western
    World! And to the country! And how there to find
    girls!

Sometimes in the country there may actually be no girls
And one must return disconsolately to the city. How-
    ever, first one should have a good and intensive
    look,
For to fail, and especially in matters of love, is
    depressing
And depression eats the heart away and makes one less
    able to love.
Oysters, clams, steak, anything with a high protein
    content
Is good for one's sexual powers, since semen is all
    protein;
For the feeling part, self-confidence, joy, and a tender
    and passionately loving heart!
How can girls stay away from you? They will have to
    find you
If you are like that! But what if they do not know you
    exist?

So—in the country, WALK! circulate, cover as many
  square inches of the area as you can
So that female eyes can see you, even if they are hidden
  behind ramparts of hay
Or cow barriers, pig barriers, hog barriers, chicken
  barriers, bull barriers,
Even peering out from between the interstices of a
  barn. Once they see you
They will love you, if your radiance shines in your face
(For this there are chemical preparations, but natural-
  ness is best)
And they will tentatively come out to meet you. Here,
  immediate love-making is best
Because of lack of places to go, chance of the angry
  farmer, etcetera,
But this may be dealt with later. In Turkey, in the
  country,
Sling your girl under a camel, and have her there. You
  will thrill gently
And greatly as the camel trots down the road toward
  the mill,
Where you will be thrown amidst the raw grain. You
  must immediately escape
Or you'll be ground to bits! And take the girl off with
  you
For she may later come to be the one that you will love,
Which you cannot do if she is in a thousand pieces, or
  even in fifteen
Or three. One man once loved a girl who was in two

But that was a rare occasion and does not affect the
more general behavior
That is the subject of this book. So rescue the girl. In
any case,
Even if you do not love her later, you will, I feel sure,
Enjoy making love that once after escaping from death.

For meeting girls, then, in the country, the rule is BE
SEEN.
In the city, GO WHERE THEY ARE. In Turkey, or
any foreign country,
TRAVEL WITH THEIR CUSTOMS OF LIFE, as
with the incident of the camel.
Having found the woman, however, what can you say?

Or what if she runs past you, fleetingly, at the beginning
of night?

3

Of course you must stop her. Say anything: "Hello!"
"Good-bye!"
Anything to arrest her attention, so that when her pace
is slowed
She will be able to listen to you and be totally
entranced by you,
So that later she will be with you, all breasts and
fragrance!

And what you say should not merely win over the woman
But add to the zest and to the glory of everything you do.

Sweet is making love out of doors, and making love on walls
Built to surround ancient cities, sweet being close to a girl beneath overhead highways
Or in a downtown sunlit hotel, from which afterwards you walk out and look at the statues
Of the city, at the main piazza, and the opera dome. And sweet it is if you have engraved your name
Or written it or stamped it on your girl's thigh, to walk on mirrored floors
So you can see it. And it is a great pleasure
To have your girl riding on a wagon and you run after her
And catch her and pull her down and make love on the road in the dust.
Sweet the first contact of bodies—and one of the sweetest things in life is to talk to someone
Delicious and unavailable and to wholly win her over by what you say!

When you first see a woman you do not know, some time, some autumn, Septembery
Day when the leaves are making curtains through which the gargoyles peer

At you as you are standing there astonished by that
   ivory and those hooks
You imagine to be holding all together without which
   she would be naked and in your arms,
As you stand there thinking of that, you may find
   yourself speechless
From so much excitement! In such situations, one
Thing you can usually rely on is asking for directions—
To someplace, to be sure, which you cannot find unless
   she goes with you,
And of course you should have some room along the
   way
To which you can take her. And it is a good idea in
   most cases also
To ask for directions to places that are likely to excite
   the
Woman you are asking them of, such as "Where is the
   Duomo of Ropes?" or
"In what museum is the Daumier painting of the girl
   who is rolling like a wheel?"

If you pretend a woman is someone you already know,
An already existing girlfriend, lost love, former student,
   and so on, that is also a good way to
Begin, and you can start in talking at once in a relaxed
   and
Intimate way, which is a joy in itself. And if you pretend
   to know a woman, you can kiss her
At once, which is always an excellent idea. Not only
   does doing so

Sometimes bring instant success, but it also prepares the way

For possible future encounters, as does thoughtful praise—

For the well-placed compliment, like an Easter egg, beautiful but hidden,

Can influence a woman, as a kiss can, for years of her life.

In general, you should kiss as many women as you can,

Taking any excuse to do so: pretending you know her, saying

Hello or good-bye to her, seeing her at a parade, at a party, and so on.

In train stations, kiss any pretty girl in sight. A friendly kiss may implant in a girl the idea

That she would like to see you again. Then who knows what may happen?

Compliments may be 1) whispered as the girl walks past you

2) stated to her directly, as you move into her path, then bow as she goes by you

3) read into a dictaphone and played as woman after woman comes along

4) given when you do not know the woman at all
   5) given after one minute's acquaintance

6) after two 7) after three. The "striking" compliment, i.e. with which to

Win the one one does not know should not be delayed
    beyond approximately
Three minutes, unless some other potent factor is
    having an effect—your
Being famous, excessively good-looking, or covered with
    precious jewels
Or being accompanied by an interesting gigantic ani-
    mal, i.
E., anything that will make talk easy because of
    astonishment
Or admiration—but even in these cases you should
    quickly come to praise
Because it is so moving and love makes it so natural a
    thing to do.

In regard to content, compliments are of six types,
    reducible to three
Chief ones, which are Compliments to the Body—in-
    cluding of course the face,
The coloration, and the movements; Compliments to
    the Mind—for
Lack of a better term, considered to include the
    sensibility
As a whole, sensitivity in particular, deep understand-
    ing, and
Comprehension of details; and Compliments to Some-
    thing Else—whatever
Doesn't go in One or Two, such as ability to fire clay
    sculptures, arrange flowers,

Or behavior and elegance in general. Under this last
   could come
Moral or characterological praise, though this might be
   considered as being in Category Two.
The essence of the compliment, of whatever type it is
You give the woman, if it is to give you the maximum
Benefits of her enjoyment and passion for you, and if
   you are to
Like giving it, as one may like giving the world a poem,
A symphony, or a bridge, is that it be free, a free
   possession
Of the woman or girl that you give it to, in other words
   that she
Feels no obligation to respond (though I assure you that
   she will)
And feels free to wear it entirely on her own. Then she
   will turn to you
With happy and returning desire. Of all compliments
   there
Are two kinds: those which show desire, and those
   which do not. "You look Etruscan!"
Is a good example of the compliment without desire
(Apparently) and "You look so delicious I want to bite
   you! My God, you drive me
Crazy!" is an example of the other kind. In the one case
   the woman is left with
A high historic feeling and feeling her beauty is
   somehow eternal,
That she shares in an eternally beautiful type

95

Away from the sphere of our sorrow, and thus that her
     life must somehow mean something
And she be an achievement of some marvelous kind
     (which she is), and the other, more
Earthy-seeming compliment makes her feel a happy
     object of desire,
The source of fervid feeling in others, a sort of
     springtide or passage of time,
Or else a Venus, or else a sunrise, or sunset, the cause of
     sleepless evenings and gasps
(This compliment is not demanding, because it is
     exaggerated
And humorous in being that, and lets the woman
     decide).

Everything about love makes people feel in a more
     intense way,
So it seems natural enough to start right in, with "You
     are beautiful
As a) Botticelli's Venus, or b) a slice of angelfood cake,
     I want
To devour you—for my sweet tooth is the ruling tooth
     of my life!"

Later you can cry to her, when alone with her, "Oh you
     are the enslaving of me,
Dear sweet and irrefutable love!" And when you are
     dancing with her
Or anywhere in public, you may even wish to praise her

In a secret language which no one else will under-
  stand—
"Gah shlooh lye bopdoosh," for example, may mean
  "Your left leg
Is whiter even than the snow which on Mount Kabana-
  yashi
Tops all Japan with its splendor!" and "Ahm gahm
  doom bahm ambahm glahsh": "I
Would like to tie you to this bannister and
Kill you with my kisses all night!" For if you believe
There is a magic in love, to get to it you will go to any
  extremes.

And one goes on looking, and talking. And neither the
  tongue
Nor the eyes wear out, and the streets are filled with
  beautiful breasts and words.

One excellent thing to do once a woman will listen to
  you
Is to read her poems, and the best of all poems to read
  is this one,
Accompanied, if you like, by acting out its details.
  Which now let us continue.

For there are numerous questions remaining which one
    must consider
If one is serious about love and determined to learn all
    its ways.

What is Love's Ideal City? what strange combination
Of Paris and Venice, of Split for the beauty of its
    inhabitants,
Of Waco for its byways, of Vladivostok for its bars?
What, precisely, is meant by the "love of God"? or the
    "love of humanity"?
How can girls best be conquered in different cities?
What places, or bits of landscape, most speak of love?
How to make your girlfriend into an airplane, or a living
    kite;
How to convert success in business or art into success in
    love;
Keeping one's libidinous impulses at a peak all the time;
How to explain, and how to prosper with having two
    loves, or three, or four, or five;
Meeting women, disguised, in museums, and walking
    with them, naked, in the country;
How to speak of love when you do not know the
    language; how to master resentment;
How to cause all the women eating in a given restaurant
    to fall in love with you at the same time;
Greek aphrodisiac foods, how to eat them and how to
    prepare them;

One secret way to make any woman happy she is with you;

Apollo: woman-chaser, homosexual, or both? Zeus: godlike ways of seducing women;

How to judge the accuracy of what you remember about past love;

Building a house ideally suited to love; how to reassure virgins;

How to avoid being interested in the wrong woman; seven sure signs of someone you don't want to love;

Three fairly reliable signs of someone you do;

Use of the car—making love under the car; in the car; on the car roof;

Traveling with women; what to do when suddenly you know that the whole relationship is no longer right;

How to pump fresh air into the lungs of a drowned girl; the "kiss of death"; how to appear totally confident and totally available for love at the same time;

Maintaining good looks under exhausting conditions; forty-one things to think about in bed;

How to win the love of a girl who is half your age; how to win the love of one who is one fifth your age;

Bracelets women like to have slipped onto them; places in which women are likely to slip and thus fall into your arms;

The bridge of ships: how to make love there in twenty-five different positions

So as to have a happy and rosy complexion later, at the "Captain's Table";

Love in different cultures: how to verify what you are
feeling in relation to the different civilizations of
the world—
Room for doubt: would the Greeks have called this
"love"? Do such feelings exist in China?
Did they exist in Ming China? and so on. The Birthday
of Love—
On what day is Eros's birthday correctly celebrated?
Was love born only once?
Is there actually a historical date? Presents to give on
such a day;
What memorable thing did Spinoza say about love?
How to deal with the sweethearts of your friends
When they want to go to bed with you; how to make
love while asleep;
The Book of Records, and what it says; how to end a
quarrel;
How to plan a "day of love"—what food and drink to
have by your side, what newspapers and books;
How to propose the subject so that your girlfriend will
go away with you
On a "voyage to the moon," i.e. lie under the bed while
you
Create a great hole in the mattress and springs with
your hatchet
And then leap on her, covered with feathers and shiny
metal spring
Fragments, screaming, as you at last make love, "We
are on the moon!" How to dress
Warmly for love in the winter, and coolly in the sun;

Mazes to construct in which you can hide naked girls and chase them;

Dreams of love, and how they are to be interpreted;

How "love affairs" usually get started; when to think of marriage; how to prevent your girl from marrying someone else;

"Magical feelings"—how to sustain them during a love affair; traveling with a doctor

As a way to meet sick girls; traveling with a police officer as a way to meet criminal girls;

What is "Zombie-itis"? do many women suffer from it? how can it be enjoyed

Without actually dying? where are most adherents to it found?

What ten things must an older man never say to a young woman?

What about loving outdoors? what good can we get there from trees, stones, and rivers?

Are there, in fact, any deities or gods of any kind to Love?

And if so, can they be prayed to? Do the prayers do any good?

What can be done to cure the "inability to love"? senseless promiscuity? twenty-four-hour-a-day masturbatory desires?

What nine things will immediately give anyone the power to make love?

What three things must usually be forgotten in order to make love?

Ways of leaving your initials on girls; other "personaliz-
ing insignia";

How to turn your girl into a duck, turkey, or chicken,
for fifteen minutes;

What to do when she comes back to herself, so she will
not be angry or frightened;

How to make love while standing in the sea; cures for
"frozen legs"; Love's icebox;

Love Curses to blight those who interfere with you, and
Love Charms to win those who resist you;

Traveling while flat on your back; Girls from Sixteen
Countries; what to do with a Communist or other
Iron Curtain Country Girl

So that politics will not come into it, or will make your
pleasure even greater;

How to identify yourself, as you make love, with
sunlight, trees, and clouds;

What to do during a Sex Emergency: shortage of girls,
lack of desire, absence of space in which to sit or lie
down;

How to really love a woman or girl for the rest of your
life; what to do if she leaves you;

Seventeen tried and tested cures for the agonies of lost
love;

Telling a "true" emotion from an in some way "untrue"
one;

How to compensate for being too "romantic"; can
enjoyed love ever come up to romantic expecta-
tions?

Ways of locating women who love you in a crowd;
   giving in totally to love;
How to transform a woman into a "Human Letter"
By covering her with inscriptions, which you then ship
   to yourself
In another bedroom, unwrap it, read it, and make love;
Making love through a piece of canvas; making love
   through walls;
What to do when one lover is in a second-floor
   apartment, the other in the first-floor one;
Openings in the ceiling, and how to make them; how to
   answer the question
"What are you doing up there on the ceiling?" if
   someone accidentally comes home;
Ways to conceal the fact that you have just made love
   or
Are about to make love; how to explain pink cheeks,
   sleepiness.
Is love all part of a "Great Plan," and, if so, what is the
   Plan?
If it is to keep the earth populated, then what is the
   reason behind that?
Throwing your girl into the ocean and jumping in after
   her, aphrodisiac effects of; genius,
Its advantages and disadvantages in love; political
   antagonism in love:
She is a Moslem, you are a Republican; or she is a
   Maoist, and you are for improving the system;
How to keep passion alive while beset by anxiety and
   doubt;

What is the best way to make love in a rocket? what is
the second-best way?

How to make sure one's feeling is "genuine"; how to use
gags; when to wear a hat;

At what moment does drunkenness become an impedi-
ment to love?

What is the role of sex in love? Is fidelity normal? Are
all women, in one sense, the same woman?

How can this best be explained to particular women?
Drawing one's portrait on a woman's back—

Materials and methods; is growing older detrimental to
love?

Use of the aviary; use of the kitchen garden; what are
eighteen totally unsuspected enemies of love?

Does lack of love "dry people up"? how can one be sure
one's love will be lasting?

What reasonable substitute, in love's absence, could be
found for love?

The best authors to consult about love (aside from the
author of this

Volume) are Ovid, Ariosto, Spenser, and Stendhal.
Places or bits of landscape

Which most speak of love: Piazzale Michelangelo,
looking down at the Arno, above Florence;

The candy factory in Biarritz, specializing in ruby-red
hearts;

Gus's Place, in Indonesia, a small cart-wheel store full of
white paper; the Rotterdam Harbor on an April
evening.

The Ideal City for Love—should be a combination

Of Naples, for its byways and its population and its Bay; Paris

For everything except the stinginess of some of its inhabitants;

Rome, for its amazement, not for its traffic; Split, for its absence of the Baroque;

Austin, Texas, for having so many pretty girls there; Eveningtown, Pennsylgrovia, for being completely unknown,

So no one can come in to spoil the lovification, although many can and do come in

And are swept up into it entirely, I will tell you later, if I remember, how to get there;

Shanghai, for the unusability of its streets; Hangkow, for its evenings; Phoenix, for its temperature

On autumn evenings; Mexico City, for its Fragonard-esque rose

Of bullfights! the caped hat! the paseos! And the magic Aspirin tablet of Capesville, Georgia,

Where no one lives; Easter Island City, for the uncloistered quality of its inhabitants; Thailand Chonk,

For the bittersweet lemons sold at its fair; and Egg-Head, Florida, for its stones.

This ideal city of love will not be as spread out

As London is, or as over-towering as New York, but it will be a city. Suburbs are inimical to love,

Imposing the city's restrictions without its stimulation and variety.

The city must include numerous girls. Therefore city
    planners
Will include as many colleges as they can and encour-
    age
Such professions as will draw young women to the city
    from outside.

To make your girl into an airplane, ask her to lie down
    on a large piece of canvas
Which you have stretched out and nailed to a thin
    sheet of aluminum, or, if you are economizing, of
    balsa wood.
When she has lain down, wrap the stuff she is lying on
    around her
And ask her to stretch out her arms, for these will be the
    wings
Of the plane (she should be lying on her stomach), with
    her neck stretched taut, her chin
Resting on the canvas (her head should be the "nose" of
    the plane); her legs and feet should be
Close together (tied or strapped, if you like). Now, once
    she is in airplane position,
Wrap the aluminum or balsa-coated canvas more
    closely around her and fasten it at the edges
With staples, glue, or rivets. Carry her to the airport, or
    to any convenient field,
And put her on the ground. Ask her to "take off!" If she
    does, you have lost a good mistress. If not
(And it is much more likely to be "if not"), you will
    enjoy making love there on the field—

You, both pilot and crew, and passengers, and she your
 loving plane!

Perhaps you would also like to turn your girl into a shoe
 or into a shoebox
Or a plaster cherry tree or any one of a million other
 things. A booklet is coming out
Specifically and entirely on that, called *The Shop of
 Love*.

The best way to conquer girls in different cities is to
 know the mayor or ruler of the particular city
And have him introduce you to the girls (perhaps while
 they are under the influence of a strong love-mak-
 ing drug).

To revive an old love affair, write the woman con-
 cerned, or call her up. Suggest converting her into a
 plane.
If she loves you still, she'll hesitate or say yes. If she says
 no, propose converting her into the summer dawn.

To cause all the women in a given restaurant to wish to
 make love to you,
Bring in the model of an airplane and stare at it
 attentively and refuse to eat.

You can tell a woman's character by looking in her shoe,
 if you have the special glasses described in *The
 Shop of Love*.

Otherwise, the eyes, mouth, and breasts are better
indications.
If the breasts are round, she may be foolish; if the eyes
are green, she may be Jewish;
If the mouth is full, she may be pettish. But everything
she is will be for you.

The wrong woman can be identified by the following
characteristics:
She eats at least twice as much as you do; her shoes or
clothing are unbuttoned or untied; she dislikes cold
water;
Her face is the shape of a donkey's; she fears evening
For evening draws one closer to bed. She contradicts
herself
And is stubborn about each thing she said. She is
perpetually unhappy
And would hate you bitterly for changing her condition.
Immediately leave her! This person is not for you!

Two signs of love-worthiness in a woman are climbing
to the roof
Without fear and with a smile on her face; turning
around to look at you after she turns away from
you.

Use of the car is now located in *The Shop of Love*.

When you know the relationship is not right, think of it
all again.

Try again the next day. If you still think the same thing,
   end it.

The kiss of death is currently prohibited by law. Look
   for it in later editions.

To maintain good looks under exhausting conditions,
   think about an eskimo
Riding a white horse through a valley filled with falling
   other eskimos
So that he always has to be attentive, so that no eskimo
   falls on his head.
This will give you an alert look, which is half of beauty.

One thing to think about in bed is the full extent of this
   poem.
Another is the city of Rome. Another is the Byzantine
   stained-glass window showing Jesus as a human
   wine-press.
Do not think of cancellation of air trips, botched tennis
   racquets, or slightly torn postage stamps.
Think of the seasons. Think of evening. Think of the
   stone duck
Carved by the cement company in Beirut, to advertise
Their product. Think of October. Do not think of
   sleep.

To win the love of a girl half your age, add your age and
   hers together

And divide by two; act as if you were the age repre-
sented by that number
And as if she were too; the same with girls one fourth or
one fifth your age.
This is called "Age Averaging," and will work in all
those cases
In which age difference is a problem. Often it is not.

Love between living beings was unknown in Ming
China. All passion was centered on material things.
This accounts for the vases. In Ancient Greece there
was no time for love. In Somaliland only little
children love each other.

Spinoza's remark was "Love is the idea of happiness
attached to an external cause."

Friends' sweethearts should be put off until the next
day.

To make love while asleep, try reading this book. It has
been known to cause Somnamoria.

The Book of Records says the record number of times a
man made love in a twenty-four-hour period was
576 times.
The record number of times a woman made love was
972 times.
The man died, and the woman went to sleep and could
not be awakened for two years.

She later became the directress of a large publishing house and then later in life became a nun.

The most persons anyone ever made love to in rapid succession (without a pause of any kind) was seventy-one.

Dreams about love should be acted on as quickly as possible

So as to be able to fully enjoy their atmosphere. If you dream about a woman, phone her at once and tell her what you have dreamed.

Zombie-itis is love of the living dead. It is comparatively rare.

If a woman likes it, you can probably find other things she likes that you will like even more.

Ten things an older man must never say to a younger woman:

1) I'm dying! 2) I can't hear what you're saying! 3) How many fingers are you holding up?

4) Listen to my heart. 5) Take my pulse. 6) What's your name?

7) Is it cold in here? 8) Is it hot in here? 9) Are you in here?

10) What wings are those beating at the window?

Not that a man should stress his youth in a dishonest way

But that he should not unduly emphasize his age.

The inability to love is almost incurable. A long sea
   voyage
Is recommended, in the company of an irresistible girl.

To turn a woman into a duck, etc., hypnotize her and
   dress her in costume.
To make love standing in water, see "Elephant Con-
   gress" in the *Kama Sutra* (chap. iv).
During a shortage of girls, visit numerous places; give
   public lectures; carry this volume.

Lost love is cured only by new love, which it usually
   makes impossible.
Finding a girl who resembles the lost girl may offer
   temporary relief.

One test for love is whether at the beginning you are or
   are not able to think about anything else.

To locate unknown-about love for you in a woman in a
   crowd,
Look intently at everyone you find attractive, then fall
   to the ground.
She will probably come up to you and show her
   concern.

Railway Express will not handle human letters, but
   Bud's Bus and Truck Service will.

Sleepiness may be explained by drugs; pink cheeks, by
the allergy that caused you to take them.

Love being part of a Great Plan is an attractive idea
But has never been validated to anyone's complete
satisfaction.

Throwing your girl in the ocean makes her feel sexy
when she gets out. Genius is not a disadvantage.

Hats should never be worn when making love. All
women are not the same woman
Though they sometimes seem so. The aviary is best used
on summer nights. There is no
Substitute for or parallel to love, which gives to the
body
What religion gives to the soul, and philosophy to the
brain,
Then shares it among them all. It is a serious matter.
Without it, we seem only half alive.

May good fortune go with you, then, dear reader, and
with the women you love.

ABOUT THE AUTHOR

KENNETH KOCH's books of poetry include *The Pleasures of Peace, Thank You,* and *Ko, or A Season on Earth.* He is also the author of *Wishes, Lies, and Dreams: Teaching Children to Write Poetry; Rose, Where Did You Get That Red? Teaching Great Poetry to Children;* and *A Change of Hearts: Plays, Films, and Other Dramatic Works.* He lives in New York City and teaches at Columbia University.